The Power and Glory of Prayer

"And as he was praying, the appearance of his face changed, and his clothing became dazzling white."
(Luke 9:29)

By

Jennifer Nakuda

All scripture quotations in this book are taken from the King James Version of the Bible, unless otherwise indicated

First printing 2021

Second printing 2025

USA Contact:
Tel: +1 945 304 3959
Email: jeniffern2000@gmail.com
Visit My social media:
Instagram: Jennifer Nakuda Author
Facebook: Jennifer Nakuda Author

Miracle Center Embassy
Arua, Uganda
Tel: +256 772612656, +256 703656873,
Email: franknankunda@gmail.com

Copyright © 2021

Dedication

I humbly take this grand opportunity to appreciate the man of God, who has had the greatest influence upon our lives, and ministry through the years, Rev. Chris Oyakhilome, DSc., DD. Thank you dear man of God for always teaching us the timeless truth of God's word in its simplest form; hearing you has brought out the best of God in us. We are forever grateful to God for you, sir. We love you dearly and pray for you always.

Acknowledgments

This book wouldn't be possible without the overwhelming inspiration of the Holy Spirit. What a privilege and an honor we have as children of God to pray and make necessary changes by the Holy Spirit in the name of Jesus. There is no other life I would rather live than this in Christ Jesus.

I'm grateful to every one of you dear children of God that I have an opportunity to pray with through the years. I have been tremendously blessed and built up during our moments of prayer, both learning from you all and sharing the glorious experiences of prayer and the answers to our prayers. God bless you all for me!

A big thank you to Bookwave Publishing for a job well done in refining my words, designing the cover page, and publishing a beautiful piece of work.

And of course, a mega thank you to my dear husband for the unwavering support always.

About the Author

Jennifer Nakuda is an ordained pastor and co-founder, alongside her husband, Frank Nakuda, of Miracle Embassy Church in Uganda, East Africa. Since 2003, she has served in various capacities within the church ministry. Inspired by her interactions with people from all walks of life, Pastor Jennifer has authored six books, offering practical guidance on living a purposeful and fulfilling Christian life. Outside of her ministry work, she is inspired by the beauty of the natural environment, enjoys traveling, and values quality time with family and friends.

Let us connect on Facebook and Instagram, or via email: jeniffern2000@gmail.com

Table of Contents

Introduction

Jesus once told a parable of how men ought always to pray and not to faint, saying, *"There was in a city a judge which feared not God, neither regarded man; and there was a widow in that city and she came unto him saying, avenge me of mine adversary. And he would not for a while; but afterward he said within himself though I fear not God, nor regard man; yet because this widow troubles me, I will avenge her, lest by her continual coming she weary me. And the Lord said hear what the unjust judge saith. And shall not God avenge his own elect which cry day and night unto him though he bear long with them? I tell you that he will avenge them speedily. Nevertheless when the son of man cometh, shall he find faith on the earth?"* (Luke 18:1-8)

Jesus made it clear in this parable that no matter the situation, God is always more than ready to answer the prayers of his children. Unlike the unjust Judge, God does not answer our prayers because we have wearied him for long. As a matter of fact, He answered all our prayers by sending Jesus Christ to pay for our sins and make us children of God. *"And if children then heirs; heirs of God and joint-hers with Christ."* (Rom 8:17)

God is however, always concerned about the state of his children's faith. For example, before we ever start to pray, are we aware that we are heirs of God and joint-heirs with Christ and that all things are ours in Christ (1 Cor 3:21)

Our faith in what God has made us in Christ unlocks the miracle-working power of God in us. Faith in prayer is like cashing in a cheque knowing there is money for you in the bank. Although your national bank may run out of cash, our inheritance in Christ never runs dry. Hallelujah!

God expects us to pray and not to lose heart or give up on any matter that requires divine intervention because as children of God and heirs of God, we have the right to pray and receive answers. If you want a change, that change is possible. Just imagine a man dead and buried for four days, and Jesus walked to his tomb and called him out. Jesus stood in front of the tomb and all they heard him say was, *"Father, I thank you because you heard me. And I know that you hear me always..."* (John 11:41).

Jesus received news while in a different town that his friend Lazarus of Bethany was sick and the bibles says, *"When Jesus heard that he said, this sickness is not unto death but for the glory of God that the son of God might be glorified thereby."* (John 11:4) However, two days later Lazarus died. Jesus didn't waste time asking what on earth happened? Oh Father! How and why did Lazarus die? He instead told his disciples, let's go and wake Lazarus up. Jesus knew the Father always hears him when he prays. Lazarus' eventual death was not going to change anything rather, it was a platform for greater glory to be revealed.

Jesus showed it plainly that if God is your father, you can ask for anything and have it, regardless of how dead the situation may appear. Even if it means going against the natural laws, with unwavering faith in the Father to answer you as his heir and a joint heir with Christ, you will surely have a testimony. Didn't Jesus say *"whatsoever ye shall ask in my name, that will I do, that the father may be glorified in the son? If ye shall ask any thing in my name, I will do it."* (John 14:13-14) that's a blank cheque for you and me to fill in whatever we want at any time.

Jesus proved the power of prayer on many occasions during his earthly ministry. It was his custom to spend nights in prayer and demonstrate the power during the day. See how unwavering faith handled Lazarus' case to the glory of God. Just like Jesus, we are not expected to let any situation overwhelm us; rather, we should overwhelm the situation with our unwavering faith in the power of God to change anything.

Look at what Jesus said in John 14:12, *"verily verily, I say unto you, he that believes on me, the works that I do shall he do also: and greater works than these shall he do, because I go unto my father."* Going to His father meant sending us the Holy Spirit to come and live in us, who is the power and the doer of God's work. (John 14:16-17) In the same way, Jesus was anointed with the Holy Ghost and with power and went about doing good; have we also been anointed with the Holy Ghost and with power to do good everywhere we are in the earth? (Acts 10:38)

The bible is full of men and women who prayed and changed situations. Their stories were written for our learning. Up till today, God is still looking for a man or a woman who believes in His miracle-working power; to pray and manifest the supernatural on the earth. John Wesley once said, "It appears like God will do nothing until we pray," it is so because prayer authorizes divine intervention in the affairs of man in his world.

Through prayer, we can change unpleasant situations and re-align destinies in our lives, as well as other people's lives, cities, and the world according to God's plan. Jesus said, *"verily I say unto you, if ye have faith as a grain of mustard seed, ye shall say unto this mountain, remove hence to yonder place; and it shall remove and nothing shall be impossible unto you"* (Matthew17:20). If we believe in the word of God, that it is what it says it is, and we do have faith in the power of the Holy Ghost resident in us, we ought to pray and not faint.

1

What is prayer?

I would love to explain prayer as a spiritual activity beyond the physical realm, where the spirit man interacts with the spirit realm to influence the course of events in man's physical world. It is that spiritual activity in which every child of God is both privileged and mandated to participate, in order to align their lives and world with God's perfect will.

Prayer has been known for centuries as communication with God, which is half-truth because prayer is more than just talking to God. This definition has robbed many of their effectiveness in prayer. Oftentimes it is assumed that once we close our eyes and open our mouths to pray, we are talking to God. That's why you hear many begging him for things he has already given them, and also commanding him to do things which they should be doing, sending him on errands as though He is their Messenger. But every serious mature Christian knows that not every time we are in prayer, we are merely talking to God.

He made us kings and priests in the earth (Rev 5:10) to ensure life in the earth aligns with His perfect plan. Jesus revealed in his prayer how important it is for God's will to be done on earth as it is in heaven. God gave the earth to man (Psalms 115:16), to dwell therein joyfully in prosperity. But the bible lets us know that the foundations of the earth are out of course (Psalm 82:5). In other words, things are not going according to plan, and that explains the chaos and troubles of life. So, God has ordained His children to address the chaos and bring order to the earth, first and foremost through prayer. *"God stands in the congregation of the mighty; he judges among the gods. How long will you judge unjustly, and show partiality to the wicked? Selah Defend the poor and fatherless; do justice to the afflicted and needy. Deliver the poor and needy; free them from the hand of the wicked. They do not know, nor do they understand; they walk about in darkness; all the foundations of the earth are unstable. I said "you are gods, and all of you are children of the Most High."* (Psalms 82:1-5)

As children of God, and gods for that matter, we are expected to do something about the chaos and troubles in our world. He gave us the power of attorney to use his name that has authority in heaven, in the earth and under the earth (Phil 2:10). Therefore, in prayer, apart from communing with God, we are obligated to deal with stubborn circumstances of life mostly influenced by demonic activities aiming at hindering God's plan in the earth.

We do understand that life is more spiritual than physical. What we see with our optical eyes is not all there is. There's a spirit world that governs the physical world we see. Everything begins in the spirit realm before it manifests in the physical. The earlier we understand this, the better for us to know why the spirit says for us to pray without ceasing (1 Thess 5:17)

To think that prayer is merely talking to God, crying and begging him for this and that, asking him to protect you and your family, is a display of spiritual ignorance and immaturity. Beyond praying for personal concerns, if any, the bible clearly shows us how God has since been entrusting man with the full responsibility of influencing events on the earth through prayer.

He says in Jeremiah 1:10 *"See I have this day set thee over the nations and over the kingdoms, to root out, and to pull down, and to destroy, and to throw down, to build and to plant."* This doesn't look like Prophet Jeremiah is going to mobilize bulldozers and machine guns to accomplish this task. Neither is he going to be talking to God, begging him to do something. God has given him an assignment, and, in the spirit, he is going to exercise spiritual authority, speaking words of power to pull down some kingdoms and nations and plant others as instructed. This sounds much like a man in spiritual warfare than one merely talking to God, begging him for help.

What about Ezekiel in the valley of dry bones? Read this beautiful story in Ezekiel 37 and see how a man in prayer prophesied over a dead army and revived it to spiritual vitality. Ezekiel was definitely not speaking to God but to a situation, commanding it to change and align with God's will as he was instructed. Today we are all sent out to our world as light and salt to make our world better. We are the solution to the problems in our world. The word to change our world is in our mouth. If we can only speak it forth. Jesus said, *"Have faith in God. For verily I say unto you, that whosoever shall say unto this mountain be thou removed and be thou cast into the sea and shall not doubt in his heart but shall believe that those things which he says shall come to pass; he shall have whatsoever he says."* (Mark 11:22-24) He didn't say ask or beg God to move the mountain; he said, 'whosoever shall say unto this mountain.' He said for us to speak to the mountain, which may be a situation affecting you, your family, nation, or the world.

Jesus said to have faith in God. The kind of faith that believes that with God, all things are possible. (Luke 1:37) And if this God is resident in you by His Spirit and has given you the power of attorney to use his name, then nothing shall be impossible unto you. (Mark 9:23). Our faith is the victory that overcomes the world (1 John 5:4). Because greater is He that is in us than he that is in the world, we ought always to pray and not faint. (1 John 4:4)

Prayer is every Christian's responsibility. In prayer we do fulfill our priestly ministry as a holy priesthood called to offer spiritual sacrifices acceptable to God. (1 Peter 2:5) We are expected to offer sacrifices of praise to God continually, which is the fruit of our lips, giving thanks to his name (Heb 13:15) for who he is, what he has done, and who he has made us in Christ. It is a celebration of his great name every time we praise and worship his name, thanking him for his goodness, lifting up our holy hands in adoration. (Psalms 63:4, Psalms 134:2, 1 Tim 2:8) The lifting of our hands is an expression of gratitude, reverence, honor, and praise to our God, which He accepts gladly and connects us to the flow of his power.

As part of our priestly ministry, we have the responsibility to pray for people. (Joel 2:17-19) This is a great privilege that should not be neglected or even taken lightly by any child of God. 1 Timothy 2:1-4 clearly spells it out for us to know that God wants us to pray for all people if we are going to live a quiet and peaceable life in all godliness and honesty. Therefore, as God's children and priests unto our God, we are honored to be participators in the kingdom business, establishing our father's purpose in the, earth firstly through prayer.

Prayer then can be described as a humble demonstration of our allegiance to God as sovereign and a loving father who is all-knowing, all-powerful, who cannot withhold any good thing from his children, to whom nothing is impossible. Prayer then becomes a deeper fellowship we are called into, that not only demonstrates God's miracle-working power but most importantly keeps changing us from glory to glory as we yield our spirit, soul, and body continually in prayer.

2

Our Father in heaven prayer

After walking with his disciples for a while, the disciples turned and asked Jesus to teach them how to pray. It is not because they had never heard of prayer or seen anybody pray or even themselves never prayed before. Yes, they had known about prayer, and being Jews and descendants of Abraham, they too had prayed always. Prayer was not a new idea. But they noticed that the Messiah actually got whatever he asked for quickly. Who wouldn't want a prayer life like that of the master? So, they asked, "Master, teach us to pray."

The master was quick to respond and told them, *"After this manner therefore pray ye; our father which art in heaven Hallowed be thy name. "Thy Kingdom come" Thy will be done in the earth as it is in heaven. Give us this day our daily bread. And forgive us our debts as we forgive our debtors. And lead us not into temptation but deliver us from evil for thine is the kingdom, and the power and the glory forever amen."* (Matt 6:9-13)

This manner of praying that the master gave to his disciple has gone down to generations as the Lord's Prayer; and many love reciting it every time they want to pray, thinking they are praying to God. But he actually told them, "In this manner pray ye," in other words, "Pray in this format." The format is what he gave them not a forever and ever prayer for all situations and generations to come. Prayer must always be in line with the present revealed truth of God's word concerning the prayer point.

The manner of prayer that Jesus gave to his disciples was effective in their day, but things have pretty much changed since the death, burial, and resurrection of Jesus Christ, which brought us out of darkness into God's marvelous light, out of bondage to Satan unto freedom in the kingdom of

God. Therefore, praying the 'Lord's prayer' as it is commonly called, will not yield results apart from making you feel good like, one who has been talking to God. But after a while, you will realize no spiritual progress and start looking for help elsewhere, as it has been for many people through the years

For example, He told them to begin with adoration and worship to God, *"our father which art in heaven Hallowed be thy name."* which we are called to do today (Heb 13:15) and will be done in all ages without end. Then, he told them to pray for **"his kingdom to come,"** which was okay at that time because he had come to bring the kingdom, and prayer was needed to establish it. But now that the kingdom has come, and it is in our hearts, we don't need to pray for it to come rather to pray for its expansion, spreading to every man's heart through the preaching of the gospel. That's why we pray for the salvation of souls everywhere, commanding the devil to let go of men's hearts and minds (2 Cor 4:4), so that they can yield to the message of the gospel to be born again and receive the kingdom. Luke 17:20-21

"Thy will be done in the earth as it is in heaven." Since the fall of man, this has been the prayer, and it is the reason we do pray, to let his will be done in the earth. The earth is full of trouble because man chose his will over God's will in the garden. The corruption in the world is a result of man going against God's will. So, we continually pray to let his will be done in the earth, to have order in our lives and our world.

"Give us this day our daily bread." Before Jesus died on the cross, this prayer was relevant, but not anymore. When man disobeyed God in the garden, the ground was cursed; in sorrow and much struggling, would man eat of the land, and the devil also acquired Adam's authority over the earth. Therefore, man's life was characterized by much toiling to meet his basic needs. But Jesus came, paid the price, defeated the devil, and ended the authority of Satan over man.

Today, everyone that believes in Jesus, has been brought into the kingdom of God where we are made heirs of God and joint heirs with Christ (Rom

8:17) giving us all the authority to reign in the earth through him (Rom 5:17). Therefore, no need to beg him for food; in Christ we have been brought into abundance, in the land of more than enough all things are ours! 1Corinthian 3:21-23 All we need to do is to align our thinking with this truth and operate the divine principles of abundance such as tithe, offerings and seeds, knowing we have inherited a blessing (1Pet 3:9) that makes rich and adds no sorrow (Prov 10:22). The blessing and abundancy consciousness attracts all the good that belongs to you.

"And forgive our debts as we forgive our debtors." This too was applicable in their day when the principle was "Do to others what you want them to do to you." Therefore, if you wanted God to forgive you, you had to forgive others first. But it is not so today. Forgiveness for the child of God is free, and it is our birthright without any condition. The blood that washed us still washes today freely (1 John 1:7). Therefore, we don't forgive others because we want our heavenly father to forgive us.

We forgive those who do wrong to us because we are born of God, and it is in our nature to forgive. As children of God, we know that unforgiveness doesn't affect the person we are refusing to forgive; rather, it endangers the one who hesitates to forgive. Unforgiveness creates a dark and evil atmosphere that attracts demonic operations in the life of the one refusing to forgive (Eph 4:26-27). We are children of the light; we therefore choose to walk in the light always. (1 John1:5 -7) The abundance of grace we have in Christ enables us to forgive all manner of wrong done to us without waiting for the offender's apology.

"And lead us not into temptation, but deliver us from evil." Firstly, God has already delivered us from evil by delivering us from Satan (Col 1:13). Secondly, God tempts no one and leads no one into temptation. *"Let no man say when he is tempted, I am tempted of God; God cannot be tempted with evil, neither tempts he any man. But every man is tempted, when he is drawn away of his own lust and enticed. Then when lust has conceived, it brings forth sin and sin when it is finished brings forth death. Do not err, my* *beloved brethren."* (James 1:13-16) James has just nailed it, letting us know that God tempts no one instead, individuals are tempted and enticed by those very things they lust after.

This portion of prayer, "lead us not into temptation, but deliver us from evil," can be mistaken to give the impression that God leads people into temptation; like some have thought that God led them into particular bad experiences to teach them a lesson or test their love for him. This is very sad because God knows your heart more than anyone; he doesn't need to test you with evil to know if you are good or bad, if you love him or not. James has clearly told us God tempts no one and can never use evil on his children. All the sickness, poverty, sorrow, pain, and evil come from the devil. Those are the works of Satan's kingdom of darkness.

This portion of the prayer implied that God should not let them be tempted but instead help deliver them from the evil one who had power over them. This prayer was very relevant because humanity was still under the dominion of Satan and desperately needed God's help. But not so anymore! We have been delivered from Satan to God (Colossians 1:13). We have received authority over Satan (Luke 10:19), and sin has no dominion over us anymore (Romans 6:1)

God delivered us from the devil and gave us the authority to cast him out every time he shows up in our lives, cities, nations, and the world. If you see or suspect any working of the devil in or around you, don't negotiate or cry, neither should you plead with the devil; just do what Jesus told us to do in Mark 16:17-18 *"And these signs shall follow them that believe; in my name shall they cast out devils."* Cast them out in the name of Jesus because you have the authority and power to do so.

Let it become a practice that before you run to any doctor or drug shop, first lay hands on yourself and command that sickness to pass out of your body; this will strengthen your faith knowing the medical treatment can deal with the symptoms all they want but you've destroyed the root cause and plucked it out of your system by the name of Jesus. Many of God's children have suffered even died simply because they surrendered their lives into the hands of some professionals whose equipment cannot diagnose a demonic activity. By the time the doctors told them, "We have done our best," the situation had gotten so bad that their faith couldn't carry them through.

Looking closely at "the Lord's prayer" that some still recite today, you will notice that what he prayed for was answered; a proof that that prayer was for that time before Jesus died and rose again to give us a new life. Therefore, continuing to recite it does not make much spiritual sense or progress.

However, we can learn from the format of prayer that Jesus taught his disciples, for example, beginning our prayers with worship and adoration to God. Then be mindful of praying for God's will concerning our lives, ministry, city, nation, and the world at the time of prayer, before bringing in the personal concerns that you may want to present before the Lord. Bottom line, our praying today should be in line with the present truth of God's word as explained in the paragraphs above.

Since Jesus' death, burial, and resurrection, we are declared not guilty through our faith in him. He has brought us into a special oneness with himself, sharing the same righteous nature and eternal life. We are no longer afar off; we have been brought in by the blood of Jesus Christ (Ephesians 2). We are a new breed of people on the face of the earth (1 Peter 2:9), living in **a new day of God's grace**, with a completely new way to pray. Hallelujah!!

When we get to know what Jesus' death and resurrection did for us, we will realize that our prayer ought to be prophetic, declaring the word of God over our lives and the situations of life.

3

Praying in the Name of Jesus

"<u>And in that day ye shall ask me nothing</u>. Verily verily I say unto you; <u>whatsoever ye shall ask the father in my name</u>, he will give it you. Hitherto have you asked nothing in my name; ask and ye shall receive that your joy may be full. These things have I spoken unto you in proverbs; but the time comes when I shall no more speak unto you in proverbs, but I shall show you plainly of the father. <u>At that day ye shall ask in my name</u>; and I say not unto you that I will pray the father for you; for the father himself loves you because ye have loved me and have believed that I came out from God." (John 16:23) Jesus talked about a day which was to come, and in that day, he said, everyone was to pray to the Father in the name of Jesus. Jesus' death, burial, and resurrection brought that 'new day' that Jesus was talking about; the day to pray in his name and receive answers. We are in that day of the church in which we are commissioned to pray for anything in the name of Jesus and receive it.

Apostle John further clarifies it saying, *"And this is the confidence that we have in him, that if <u>we ask anything according to his will</u>, he hears us; And if we know that he hears us, whatsoever we ask we know that we have the petition that we desire of him."* (1John 5:14-15) <u>According to his 'will'</u> is the key in this scripture. His will for prayer is the way he has chosen for us to pray in this new day, <u>praying in the name of Jesus</u>. That is his new 'will' concerning prayer, *"And whatsoever ye shall ask in my name that will I do, that the father may be gloried in the son. <u>If ye shall ask any thing in my name</u> I will do it."* (John 14:14) Jesus plainly revealed to us the new way of prayer and Apostle John highlights it as God's will for prayer in this day of the church.

The phrase "according to his will" in this portion of scripture doesn't imply that God has determined that you should specifically ask for a particular thing as he wants it for you, and unless you do pray for that, he won't answer you. NO! Not at all! Because in the same scripture he gives us a blank cheque saying, "...*And if we know that he hears us, <u>whatsoever we ask</u> we know that we have the petition that we desire of him.*" (1 John 5:14-15) This literary means there is no limit to what we can ask for in his name. Think about it, how could he put a limit when he has given us everything as His heirs? His will means to pray in the name of Jesus and have it met.

In this new day of the Church (Acts 4:10-12), the name Jesus is the access code for everything. In that name we were baptized into the kingdom (Matt 28:19), in that name we live, move and have our being (Acts 17:28); and whatsoever we do in word or deed, we do in the name of the Lord Jesus (Col 3:17). We, therefore, also pray in the name of Jesus as a guarantee to answered prayer.

The name of Jesus has authority in heaven, on earth, and below. The bible says, "*And being found in fashion as a man he humbled himself and became obedient unto death, even the death of the cross; Wherefore God also has highly exalted him and given him a name which is above every name; that at the name of Jesus every knee should bow, of things in heaven and things in earth and things under the earth. And that every tongue should confess that Jesus Christ is Lord to the glory of God the father.*" (Philippians 2:8-11)

It doesn't matter whose other name you may wish to pray to the Father, you will not be heard. It will only give you a good emotional feeling of being close to divinity, but not real. If all things in heaven, in the earth and under below bow to the name of Jesus, which other name would you rather pray than Jesus? If words mean anything, and the word 'all' means everything, then everything you know and don't know, bows to the name of Jesus Christ of Nazareth, in whose name we are told to pray. This is the guarantee that our prayers will be answered because everything in heaven, on earth, and under bows to the name of Jesus. This is the confidence that Apostle John wanted us to have in prayer "Everything bows to the name of Jesus."

I grew up seeing my beloved mother pray using a small book every evening before bed. And together we would kneel as she said her prayers from the book, and we both replied at the end of every sentence 'Yuda Tadeo Omutukirivu otusaabire," which is interpreted as 'Saint Judas pray for us.' This went on for some time until I didn't see her pray that way again. Of course, it wasn't working, and for many years, she never prayed again. It was much later in my early youth that I took her to my church, where she gave her life to Christ and learnt to pray correctly. It was so beautiful that in her last days before passing on to glory, she was speaking in the tongues of the Spirit. Hallelujah!

It doesn't matter how righteous someone may have been before they died, we are not told to pray in their name, much less ask them to pray for us or on our behalf. That prayer is a complete waste of time, maybe it is directed to some other god but not the Father of our Lord and Savior Jesus Christ. We have received a new way to pray in which we have full access to the Father. That is praying in the beautiful name of Jesus Christ of Nazareth.

Irrespective of where we find ourselves in this world, we have a name that is above all names. It is the most powerful name in heaven, on earth, and under in hell. We have been given the power of attorney to use it. We heal the sick with that name, cast out demons with it, call forth money with it; just mention anything and it shall be done. (John 14:14) You have got to have faith in that all-powerful name of Jesus, and all shall be well.

"Now Peter and John went up together into the temple at the hour of prayer being the ninth hour. And a certain man lame from his mother's womb was carried, whom they laid daily at the gate of the temple which is called beautiful to ask for alms of them that entered into the temple. Who seeing Peter and John about to go into the temple asked alms; And Peter fastening his eyes upon him with John said look on us. And he gave heed unto them

expecting to receive something of them. Then Peter said, silver and gold have I none; but such as I have, give I thee; <u>In the name of Jesus Christ of Nazareth rise up and walk.</u> And he took him by the right hand and lifted him up and immediately his feet and ankle bone received strength. And he leaping up stood and walked and entered with them into the temple, walking and leaping and praising God." **(Acts 3:1-9)**

Peter told the lame beggar silver and gold I don't have, but what I have I give to you. In the name of Jesus, rise up and walk and the man, lame from the womb, walked. The difference between Peter and many Christians today is a lack of consciousness; that we have an all-powerful name that can accomplish anything, anywhere, at any time. Many are too conscious of what is not available physically and forget they have a name that can produce whatever is required.

The name of Jesus was given to us as a tool or a key that gives us access to whatever we want. We don't beg with that name. We make a demand for things to be done in the name of Jesus. Just like Peter commanded the lame man to walk in the name of Jesus, he did not pray to God to heal the lame man; he commanded the lame man to walk in the name of Jesus. He exercised the authority we have in the name of Jesus to make things happen.

Asking in the name of Jesus is not a begging prayer, rather, it is exercising the power of attorney given to us to use that name and receive answers as though Jesus himself is the one asking or commanding things to happen.

The earlier we get accustomed to using the name of Jesus with understanding, the quicker we start enjoying a life of endless possibilities without limitations.

4

Praying in the spirit

"Praying always with all prayer and supplication in the spirit and watching thereunto with all perseverance and supplication for all saints." *(Eph 6:18)*

This is a very instructive verse, letting us know we ought to pray in the spirit at all times. It can only be so that we pray in the spirit because we are primarily spirit beings that have a soul and live in the body. But because some are more conscious of the physical world, they tend to approach prayer from the physical arena depending on what they see, hear, or feel. Therefore, the spirit calls our attention to the fact that we are to pray in the spirit at all times.

Praying in the spirit is going beyond the physical realm of life to the spiritual realm where you cease from praying according to what you see, hear, or feel to what the word of God says. The word of God tells us not to be conformed to the standards of this world (not to see and reason as the world does) but to be transformed by the renewing of our mind with the word of God to know God's perfect will. Romans 12:2

When we become students of the bible, our minds are renewed to know God's mind concerning the matters of life we want to pray about. Knowing God's mind is the beginning of praying in the Spirit. With God's mind you will utter words from your spirit, praying either with your spirit in other tongues or praying with the understanding in the language you know, according to God's word concerning the matter. 1 Cor 14:14 says, *"For if I pray in an unknown tongue, my spirit prays, but my understanding is unfruitful. What is it then? I will pray with the spirit, and I will pray with the understanding also: I will sing with the spirit and and I will sing with the understanding also.* This lets us know that praying in the spirit primarily is speaking in the tongues of the spirit.

Praying with your spirit is the highest level of prayer a child of God could ever make. God has so graciously enabled the new creation in Christ Jesus to pray with the spirit; speaking mysteries in other tongues or sometimes in groanings that cannot be uttered. Your mind may never understand exactly what you are saying until you receive interpretation, but your spirit is praying according to the perfect will of God concerning the matter at hand.

Praying with the spirit happens in two ways. The first one is when your spirit prays, making utterances in other tongues that are inspired of the Holy Spirit, *"For if I pray in an unknown tongue, my spirit prays..."* (1 Cor 14;14). This kind of prayer can happen anywhere and anytime once one is filled with the Holy Spirit. It is commonly referred to as praying or speaking in other tongues. From the day the person receives the utterance from the Holy Spirit, the tongues just flow at any time in prayer.

The question then might be, is speaking in tongues for every born-again Christian? Emphatically Yes! That is God's desire for all his children and a sign for the believing ones. At his resurrection, while commissioning his disciples to go into the whole world to preach the gospel Jesus said, *"__And these signs shall follow them that believe__; in my name shall they cast out devils; they shall speak with new tongues..."* (Mark 16:17) Therefore if you have believed in Jesus and confessed him as Lord and Savior of your life, you are fully entitled to speak in the tongues of the spirit. It is one of those signs that Jesus said would identify those who have believed in him! You cannot believe in him and not believe in speaking in tongues of the spirit.

Shortly before his ascension into heaven to sit at the right hand of God, Jesus told his disciples not to depart from Jerusalem until they were baptized with the Holy Spirit (Acts 1:4-5). As soon as they got filled with the Holy Spirit, the bible says they all spoke in new tongues, *"And they were __all__ filled with the Holy Ghost and began to speak with other tongues, as the spirit gave them utterance* (Acts 2:1-4). These were not only the 12 Apostles but all those who believed in Jesus and followed him up to this time. Church history says there were about 120 people in the upper room at the time that received the Holy Spirit and spoke in new tongues of the spirit.

Simply ask the Holy Spirit to give you the utterance, and go ahead and open your mouth and begin speaking. You may start with prayer or a song in the language you know, and then the tongues of the spirit may pop up from your spirit to take over your prayer. There is no formula on how to start speaking in tongues, it happens anytime, in any way, when you yield to the flow of God's Spirit.

Thousands have spoken in tongues all over the world while in prayer; others, when a minister laid hands on them to receive the Holy Spirit, and some others don't even remember how it all started. All they know is that today they speak in tongues at the snap of a finger, because it is our birthright and a sign that we have believed in Jesus Christ.

The born-again Christian is awakened to God's spiritual realm and has been brought into function from that realm of spiritual life. Don't deny yourself the many benefits we enjoy from speaking in other tongues. Take time to study the subject from the scriptures and discover for yourself this wonderful blessing of speaking in tongues given to the church of Jesus Christ to operate from a higher realm of life.

If you want to enjoy the Christian life that goes from glory to glory with tremendous impact in your world, pray in tongues more often than in any other language you know. Apostle Paul knew the secret and told the Corinthian church *"I thank my God I speak with tongues more than you all."* (1 Corinthians 14:18) Apostle Paul is that great Apostle of our Lord Jesus Christ that has helped the church to discover who we are through his deep revelations about the new creation in Christ. It is believed that, as a result of his much praying in other tongues, his spirit was enlightened and opened to see the realities of the spirit realm we live as children of God.

Groanings that cannot be uttered

The other way of praying with the spirit is when the Holy Spirit himself makes intercession with groanings that can't be articulated in words, *"Likewise, the Spirit also helps our infirmities; for we know not what we should pray for as we ought; but the Spirit himself makes intercession for us with groanings which cannot be uttered. And he that searches the hearts knows what the mind of the Spirit is because he makes intercession for the saints according to the will of God."* (Rom 8:26-27).

The Holy Spirit loves praying through us when we completely yield ourselves to him in prayer. This kind, however, doesn't just happen all the time in prayer, and we do not just sit and tell the Holy Spirit to start praying through us. This kind usually happens at His will, any time or while we are in prayer; at most when we yield to him in deep desire by creating an atmosphere that enraptures our spirit, mind, and emotions to be in sync with the Holy Spirit.

This kind of groaning has happened to many people in prayer, and because they didn't understand it, they stopped wondering what had happened to them, but this is the most effective way of praying with your spirit. Don't forget that this particular prayer of groaning is done by the Holy Spirit himself, the author of everything, the all-knowing God who has the power to alter destinies and change situations for good. Next time you find yourself in groanings that can't be uttered, continue as long as the flow is still on until the Spirit stops in victory.

Many times, we stop too soon in prayer because we planned to pray for a specific period of time. This has denied many of the permanent victories. If we release ourselves in prayer and allow the Holy Spirit to take charge, we will enjoy plenty of the benefits of prayer. From time to time, we should create enough time for fellowship with the Holy Spirit in prayer. This is what puts us over in life far ahead of others who don't give the Holy Spirit enough time. The few minutes' prayer may not always be enough for a glorious and most effective Christian life. If only we stayed a little longer in prayer, we would see the power and the glory of prayer as it should be.

Life is spiritual, and if we deal with it from the spirit realm, it will never be a mystery to us. That's why Paul says though I don't understand what I am saying in tongues, I am ok, and I will continue to pray with my spirit in tongues first and then pray with the understanding also. *"For if I pray in an unknown tongue, my spirit prays, but my understanding is unfruitful. What is it then? I will pray with the spirit and I will pray with the understanding also..."* (1Cor14:14-15). Praying with the tongues of the Holy Spirit, who knows everything, is the most effective way of praying. And then after we can pray with the understanding also, which is praying in the language we understand

Apostle Paul is letting us know that though our understanding is limited when praying in unknown tongues or with groanings; yet our prayer is most effective causing impact as we speak mysteries in the spirit realm (1 Cor 14:2) according to God's perfect will (Rom 8:26). With every manner of prayer, the Apostle spoke in tongues and advised us to do the same saying, *"And pray in the Spirit on all occasions with all kinds of prayers and requests. With this in mind, be alert and always keep on praying for all the saints."* (Ephesian 6:18 NIV)

Advantages of praying with the spirit

Praying with the spirit edifies us (1 Corinthians 14:4). To edify also means to improve, inform, and enlighten, among others. What this means is that speaking in tongues improves you, informs you, and enlightens you spiritually first, and then brings that spiritual information and understanding to your mind, so you know what you need to know at that time. You can receive information about what you are praying about in tongues, giving you a clear understanding of what needs to be done.

Praying in tongues quickens your understanding of the scriptures. The Holy Spirit is the spirit of wisdom and the author of the scriptures. He will reveal and make the scriptures real to your spirit. Speaking in tongues will open your spirit to be taught the word by the Holy Spirit. Whether you are listening to the word or studying the word of God, the understanding that will come to your spirit will be more accurate and relevant to you than the one who doesn't speak in tongues. People who have problems with the word of God are mainly those who don't spend much time praying in the tongues of the spirit.

Praying with the spirit builds you up *"But ye beloved, building up yourselves on your most holy faith, praying in the Holy Ghost."* (Jude 1:20). Now this is where the secret of building our faith strong is found. After you have read the scriptures, and your faith is inspired to do the impossible, praying in tongues will cause the word to sink deeper in your spirit, empowering your faith and building it higher and stronger. It is from this spiritual height of your faith that you will start declaring those things you have believed, and they will be established for you, and no force in the universe can stop you because the word is now rooted and mingled with your spirit, ready to give you what it talks about.

Praying with the spirit will lead you into your life purpose. Every one of us has a specific God given life purpose which many never live to fulfill because they never get to know or choose to do. But praying in the spirit will help you realize your purpose in life and energize you to fulfill it. While praying in the spirit, the Holy Spirit may specifically speak to you about your purpose or lead you into that purpose where you find yourself doing that purpose with joy and commitment that could never have been possible without the help of the Holy Spirit. *"Howbeit when he the Spirit of truth is come, he will guide you into all truth: for he shall not speak of himself; but whatsoever he shall hear, that shall he speak and he will show you things to come.* (John 16:14)

The bible warns us to, *"Never lag in zeal, and in earnest endeavor, be aglow and burning with the spirit, serving the lord."* (Romans 12:11 AMP) Those who speak in tongues often, never have a dull day. They are always full of life, vibrant and not only optimistic about life, but always full of fresh ideas. They know no limitations. They turn every challenge into an opportunity to touch lives and make Jesus famous. They stay inspired and motivated about those things they know they are supposed to do; just like Paul prayed for the brethren at Ephesus. *"That he would grant you according to the riches of his glory to be strengthened with might by his spirit in the inner man."* (Eph 3:16)

Praying with the spirit stirs up the gifts and spiritual blessings of God in you *"wherefore I put thee in remembrance that thou stir up the gift of God, which is in thee by the putting on of my hands."* (2Tim 1:6). God has blessed us with so many spiritual blessings as his children and here Apostle Paul is showing us how to activate them at any time; and one of the ways to activate them is by praying with your spirit in tongues. Those blessings and gifts of God are within your spirit. Speaking in tongues will turn them on to the glory of God. Take, for example, when you want to make a very crucial decision and you are not sure of the truth about the matter, speaking in tongues will activate the wisdom of God in you by the Holy Spirit, and you will be rightly guided on what to do.

Praying in tongues will vitalize your physical body, bringing about total wellness in your entire system and getting rid of the infections, diseases, and weakness. (Romans 8:11) This is how we live in divine health daily, refusing our bodies to be ravaged by any disease or infection, because the power of the Holy Spirit is ministered to our bodies while speaking in other tongues.

Speaking in tongues sustains you into the realm of the spirit where you were born in Christ, enabling you to participate in the spiritual happenings, enjoying the privilege to know things and influence them before they happen in the physical realm. Though your mind may not have understood what you were saying with your spirit, in the spirit you made changes, aligned destinies, stopped calamity and so many things. Hence forth your life just keeps going from glory to glory, you find yourself dealing wisely in the affairs of life, always on top and far better than anyone who doesn't speak in tongues.

There are several benefits of praying with the spirit that can't be exhausted. The list is open for everyone to add their personal experience praying in the Holy Ghost.

5

Praying with the understanding.

"What is it then? I will pray with the spirit and I will pray with the understanding also..." (1Cor14:15). Praying with the understanding is praying in the language that you understand very well; speaking words you know and attach meaning to. This is the kind of prayer most people are familiar with. They always open their mouth to pray in their language based on what they have seen, heard, or known, and may be purely from their human understanding of the situation.

However, praying with understanding goes beyond just language to understanding the revealed truth about the situation in the scriptures. Just because you prayed doesn't mean you said what was supposed to be said in your prayer. There is a way to pray for the new creation in Christ, who is a child of God, an heir of God, and a joint heir with Christ (Romans 8:17).

A full understanding of the revealed truth of the gospel of Christ makes our prayer effective. When you know you are an heir of the monarch of the universe, and you have the name (Jesus) above every name to use to your advantage, how should your prayer be like? When you know, according to the scriptures, that all things are yours (1 Cor 3:21) and you have been raised together with Christ and made to sit together in the heavenly places in Christ (Eph 2:6), and the devil has been put under your feet. How should your prayer be like?

Some of God's children are either ignorant of the scriptures or just don't stop to think when beginning to pray. Many still think prayer is a religious activity we must do as Christians, simply saying what we want to say to God without paying attention to how He expects us to pray.

After sending Jesus to die for our sins and resurrecting him to give us a new life of power, dominion, and authority, he expects us to pray in a particular way that depicts our position as children in the kingdom of God, where we are all made kings and priests (Rev 1:5-6).

When we have just come to Christ, still babies in spiritual matters, we can say anything in prayer and God accepts it. However, after a while, he expects us to grow and understand how things are supposed to be done in the kingdom. That's why, after being a Christian for a while, many start to realize that their prayers are not receiving answers as the case was when they had just given their lives to Christ.

God expects us to pray as kings and priests, we are in Christ instead of merely praying according to our feelings and what we think is prayer. This is the reason why every child of God must be a student of the bible to get acquainted with the revealed truth of the gospel in order to be effective and live a successful life.

Although praying in the language we understand can still be a prayer in the spirit when it is according to the scriptures, it is limited and can be interrupted by our myopic mind. This is important to note because most situations we normally deal with in prayer have deep spiritual roots that are unknown to man. We always require deeper spiritual insight into the reality of the matter and how to best deal with it.

Therefore, Apostle Paul prefers praying with the understanding to come second in prayer because when you start out praying with the tongues of the Spirit, after a while, words will be released into your spirit. This is one way the Holy Spirit brings to your understanding what you are saying in tongues, so you know and agree with the Spirit as you speak those words out in your language to be established for you in Jesus' name. It is at that point in prayer, after speaking in tongues of the spirit for a while that you start uttering words of faith, prophecy, spiritual warfare, shouts of victory, worship, thanksgiving and laughter as the spirit inspires you. When you boldly proclaim these utterances, they are established and joy like a river wells up out of your spirit. Soon or later, it will be testimonies everywhere.

This is exactly what the prophet Joel said would happen to us in this day. *"And it shall come to pass afterward that I will pour out my spirit upon all flesh and your sons and daughters shall <u>prophesy</u> your old men shall dream dreams, your young men shall see visions; and also upon the servants and upon the handmaids in those days will I pour out my spirit."* (Joel 2:28-29) The Holy Spirit has already been poured out on all flesh; we have Him living in us. Therefore, when we start out praying with the spirit in other tongues, we begin to receive understanding of the situations we are dealing with, and utter words full of power as they are ministered to our spirit by the Holy Spirit.

We have all been made priests unto God (Rev 1:6), and the Holy Spirit of God has come to live in us to fulfill his purpose in the earth through us. When we yield to the Spirit of God as priests, God is able to accomplish so much in and through us just like he did with Ezekiel the priest, who brought life back to a dead army (Ezek 37).

As priests of God, we ought to be mindful of the fact that anytime we are in prayer, the Spirit of God is bound to do anything with us. Just like the Spirit of God carried Ezekiel in the spirit to the valley of dry bones, which was symbolic of the state in which the children of Israel were at the time, and caused him to speak words that revived them. In the same way, while in prayer, the Spirit of God can reveal situations and inspire us to speak words of power in the language we understand and bring about the desired change anywhere, anytime. (Ezekiel 37:1-14)

Prayer time is a time of power for change. The bible says, *"...the earnest (heartfelt continued) prayer of a righteous man makes tremendous power available (dynamic in its working)."* (James 5:16 AMP) It is the <u>heartfelt, continued prayer of the righteous man</u> that you are in Christ, which makes power for change available. It is you and me who have been made righteous in Christ who can pray and make changes. When we pray with the spirit, it makes a lot of difference from when we focus on praying with 'the understanding' in the language we know. Praying in the spirit enables us to pray for many situations that require prayer at the time, according to God, which our minds could have never figured out. In this way, many lives can be saved, destiny changed, cities and nations delivered from imminent danger by praying with the spirit.

Life can sometimes be filled with overwhelming challenges, and even though we want help from God, we may not know how to handle the situation in prayer. Some with heavily confused and burdened minds have ended up complaining to God, accusing him of so many things that are going wrong in their lives instead of praying. But the scripture says, *"Likewise the spirit also helps our infirmities; for we know not what we should pray for as we ought; but the spirit itself makes intercession for us with groanings which cannot be uttered. And he that searches the hearts knows what is the mind of the spirit, because he makes intercession for the saints according to the will of God."* (Romans 8:26-27)

There you have it in the scripture above. God knew everything before we came to the scene and planned to give us the Holy Spirit to help us pray in especially in moments like these. That's why the Spirit instructs us to pray in the Spirit at all times with all manner of prayer. It is therefore preferable to start out praying with the spirit and let the Holy Spirit inspire the right words to be uttered for an effective prayer time. It doesn't matter how burdened and tired you may feel when starting to pray, if you will yield to the Spirit, speaking in other tongues, before long you will be up on your feet pacing the floor speaking words of power, commanding situations to change to your favour instead of crying, feeling sorry for yourself and blaming everyone else for what is happening.

Once again, if you are yet to speak in new tongues, and you want to, it is very simple: if you are born again, ask the Father to fill you with His Holy

Spirit and give you utterance. (Luke 11:13) The father is more pleased to see you speak in tongues than you would ever want to.

If you are not yet born again, I would ask you to say the prayer at the end of this book, meaningfully from your heart, and then ask the Father for that same Holy Spirit that has baptized you into Christ, to now fill you up and give you utterance.

Then open your mouth and say whatever flows out. As you consistently continue to speak, the tongues will become bolder as the spirit leads you. Don't refuse to speak in tongues for anything; don't cheat yourself out of this heavenly blessing of effective prayer.

6

Praying with the prophetic word of God

Another way to pray in the spirit is praying the word of God, making confessions, and declarations according to the word of God. The word of God is the most authentic prophecy of our lives in Christ. It clearly shows us who we have become in Christ and what we can do. Giving our lives to Christ did not stop trouble from coming our way. As a matter of fact, we attracted more trouble from the enemy of Christ. We became his project to ensure we fail in our Christianity like he failed in his relationship with God.

But Jesus said I will build my church, and the gates of hell shall not prevail against it. (Matt 16:18) Since the inception of the church at Pentecost, the church of Jesus Christ has been marching on. Despite all the deadly opposition and persecution that has seen many killed for the gospel, the enemy has never been able and will never be able to stop or destroy the church of Jesus Christ. However, this does not stop him from attacking the church. The bible warns in 1 Peter 5:8, *"Be well balanced (temperate, sober of mind), be vigilant and cautious at all times, for that enemy of yours, the devil, roams around like a lion roaring (in fierce hunger), seeking someone to seize upon and devour."* The next verse nine, tells us exactly what to do when he shows up.

"Withstand him, be firm in faith (against his onset- rooted, established, strong, immovable, and determined), knowing that the same sufferings are appointed to your brotherhood (the whole body of Christians) throughout the world." In other words, when he shows up, resist him in the faith. What does it mean to resist him in the faith? It means to stand on the word of God, strong and unmovable.

When the devil came to Jesus in the wilderness tempting him three times, Jesus resisted him, standing strong on the word, declaring what was written contrary to what the devil was telling him to do. (Matt 4:1-11)

Just like Paul told Timothy to fight a good fight of faith, holding onto eternal life. *"Fight the good fight of the faith. Take hold of the eternal life to which you were called when you made your good confession in the presence of many witnesses."* (1 Tim 6:12 NIV) What is the fight of faith? It is the unwavering declaration of your faith against staggering opposition. It is a good fight because we have already declared the winners for the word of God never fails. If you stick to it, you will come back with a testimony. If we confessed Christ and received eternal life, the Spirit says hold onto that life of God you received. That life never fails, it cannot be defeated; whoever has it is exempted from perishing (John 3:16).

It doesn't matter the amount of attack from the devil, if you will stand strong, rooted and immovable on the word of God, declaring who you are and what God has said and done, the situation will change. The word of God is not mere words. He says, *"is not my word like as a fire? Saith the lord; and like a hammer that breaks the rock in pieces?"* (Jeremiah 23:29) There is absolutely nothing that the word of God cannot do when in the mouth of a child of God who understands the working power of the word.

The bible continues to say, *"For the word of God is quick, and powerful, and shaper than any two-edged sword, piercing even to the dividing asunder of soul and spirit, and of the joints and marrow, and is a discerner of the thoughts and intents of the heart."* (Hebrews 4:12) There you go again! Literary nothing the word of God cannot touch, change or create. It made the whole world including man therefore it is the right material to correct anything, mend or recreate anything we want. It can correct and bring back to sanity a wayward child, man, or woman. It can heal, restore, bless, beauty and build a life of anyone, any family, any community, country, or the world.

Anything we see, we know and do not know has in it the substance of the word of God because it came into existence by the word of God. *"In the beginning was the word, and the word was with God, and the word was God. The same was in the beginning with God. All things were made by him and without him was not anything made that was made,"* (John 1:1-3). This means that anything in existence today has the ability to hear the word of God and respond to it.

The word of God was given to us to say it. We study it, meditate on it to give us a new mindset in Christ, and then we speak it forth to have it manifested in our lives and our world. *"... For He Himself has said, 'I will never leave you, nor forsake you.' So, we may boldly say, 'the lord is my helper. I will not fear. What can man do to me?"* (Hebrews 13:5-6) The Lord has said it, so we should boldly say the same thing in agreement with him and have the word manifest in our lives.

Apostle Peter, in the later days of his life, wrote to the churches assuring them of the authenticity of God's word, which he called 'a more sure word of prophecy.' Pay close attention to what he says in this portion of scripture.

"Moreover I will endeavor that ye may be able after my decease to have these things always in remembrance. For we have not followed cunningly devised fables, when we made known unto you the power and coming of our Lord Jesus Christ, but were eyewitnesses of his majesty. For he received from God the father honour and glory, when there came such a voice to him from the excellent glory, this is my beloved son, in whom I am well pleased. And this voice which came from heaven we heard, when we were with him in the holy mountain. We have also a more sure word of prophecy; whereunto ye do well that ye take heed, as unto a light that shines in the dark place, until the day dawn and the day star arise in your hearts. Knowing this first, that no prophecy of the scripture is of any private interpretation, for the prophecy came not in old time by the will of man but holy men of God spoke as they were moved by the Holy Ghost." **(2 Peter 1: 15- 19)**

Apostle Peter is letting us know that we have a surer word of prophecy, to which we can hang on as unto a light that shines in the dark place, until the day dawns and the day star arise in our hearts (until we see the reality of that word in our hearts).

In other words, find scriptures that are in line with the situation you're praying about. Just like Hosea 14:2 says, "take with you words;" Make war with them in the name of Jesus. Hold onto that word of God in prayer. Let it become real to your spirit filling you with hope, joy and assurance of God's intervention; knowing that God always watches over his word to perform it. *"...for I am watching to see that my word is fulfilled."* (Jere 1:12) Declare it until the light of that word shines like a day star in your heart, giving you a note of victory.

Born to function like him

The bible lets us know that God created man in his image after his likeness to look like him and to function like him (Genesis 1;26). In Genesis 1:2, we discover that God had an ugly situation with the earth he had created. The bible says, *"And the earth was without form and void and darkness was upon the face of the deep and the Spirit of God moved upon the face of the waters."*

The world God created had become void and formless, and darkness was everywhere. Just like most situations, we seek to change in our lives. But notice what God did in verse 3 in response to the chaotic world before him. *"And God said let there be light and there was light."* Just like God addressed his ugly situation, he expects us to do the same when faced with formless situations in life.

He has given us his Holy Spirit, who is the power in us and with us to make the required changes. When we speak, the Holy Spirit of God empowers the word we speak, causing it to come to pass in the same way he caused God's word to come to pass when he spoke to the formless earth.

He says to us in Psalms 82:6, *"I have said you are gods and all of you are children of the Most High. But ye shall die like men and fall like one of the princes."* Why die like men? Because being born again, we are not mere men, we are gods; expected to function like him, and when we don't function like the gods we are, we let the situations of life affect us as if we are mere men. This is not supposed to be so. We are supposed to change the situations of life to align with God's will and purpose.

In the same Psalm 82, we see God calling on us, his people, to do something about the wickedness in our world; to defend the poor and the afflicted because the foundations of the earth are now out of course. Many are walking in darkness, not knowing what to do. As gods, he expects us to respond to the ugly situations of life and not just look on. He says, *"How long will ye judge unjustly and accept the persons of the wicked? Selah. Defend the poor and the fatherless; do justice to the afflicted and needy. Deliver the poor and needy; rid them out of the hand of the wicked. They know not, neither will they understand; they walk on in darkness all the foundations of the earth are out of course."* (Psalms 82:2-5) God expects us to put the devil where he belongs and put things in order in our families, communities, cities, and nations. We are the restraining voice of our nations to stop evil from wreaking havoc.

He has given us his word as a material for change, to speak it forth, preach it, and pray with it every time. As long as we (the church) are still in the world, we are the light and salt of the earth. God is counting on us to make our world habitable in peace and safety. His word is the tool, *"…for it is the power of God unto salvation to everyone that believes, to the Jew first, and also to the Greek. For therein is the righteousness of God revealed from faith to faith: as it is written, the just shall live by faith."* (Romans 1:16-17)

7

The prayer of the spirit of faith

Now every prayer we make is definitely a prayer of faith as God has dealt to each one of us the measure of faith through the gospel (Rom 12:3). It is that faith that drives us to prayer believing to receive answers. Otherwise, it would have been useless to embark on prayer if we didn't have faith that situations would change. The bible says *"without faith it is impossible to please him for he that comes to God must believe that he is and that he is a rewarder of them that diligently seek him."* (Hebrews 11:6). So, we have faith, and we keep growing our faith from time to time to be able to live a great and victorious Christian life.

However, there is such a thing as a spirit of faith that is a gift of the Holy Spirit, that God allows to operate in an individual at a particular time to accomplish a specific task according to his will (1 Cor 12:9). But the spirit of faith, apart from being a gift of the Holy Spirit, can also be strongly developed through a deeper continuous fellowship with the word of God. (Romans 10:17)

This spirit of faith speaks what it believes is already done. It has no considerations whatsoever. It doesn't speak so that a change will happen if God wants the change, this spirit of faith is a force; it speaks because it has the assurance that it is just as it is said, no plan B. It is that very spirit of faith that Apostle Paul talked about in 2 Corinthians 4:13 saying, *"We having the same spirit of faith, according as it is written, I believed and therefore have I spoken, we also believe and therefore speak."* This spirit of faith doesn't take a 'NO' for an answer. It will not let go until it wins. It has the assurance that it is just as God says it is. It is the kind that doesn't surrender to opposition. This spirit knows no fear, failure, or defeat, it doesn't bark off until it is as it is said.

This prayer of the spirit of faith is the kind that can happen any time as soon as faith is turned on. It is the kind that can't wait for tomorrow to split the red sea for two million Jews to crossover before the Egyptian army takes them back to bondage (Exodus 14:15). It is that prayer that Joshua made that stopped the sun for twelve hours until he finished his enemies in war (Joshua 10:12-13). It is the same prayer that Elijah prayed for rain, and it rained the same day in Israel after three and half years of no rain (1 Kings 18:41-46). I call it the 'now faith' prayer.

It is usually stirred up by holy anger demanding an immediate change. When the spirit of faith is fully stirred up; it doesn't matter that the problem has been around for years, it doesn't matter that the whole family, village or country has the same problem and now it is heading towards you; the spirit of faith doesn't consider the source of the problem, it knows one thing, if it is not supposed to be, then it must bow to the name of Jesus now. (Phil 2:8-9)

The reason for the study of God's word is for us to see life as God sees it. To have a mindset of a winner and victor, to whom nothing is impossible. If we will be disciplined enough to study God's word, and have the word renew our minds, taking out all the fear, worry and anxiety, we will have the spirit of faith operating in our lives at all times and be able to do exploits for the kingdom.

8

Prayer of agreement

"Again, I say unto you, that if two of you shall agree on earth as touching anything that they shall ask, it shall be done for them of my father which is in heaven. For where two or three are gathered together in my name, there am I in the midst of them." (Matthew 18: 19- 20) God has not left any stone unturned concerning prayer and receiving answers. Among the many ways to make the required changes in life is the prayer of agreement with others.

The prayer of agreement is one of the most effective, depending on how it is handled. It only requires a minimum of two people on earth, agreeing on the same thing, and praying to the Father in heaven.

Agreement is the key in this prayer. The situation must be explained very well to the team members; why they should pray, how to pray, and the expected results. This gets everyone involved to agree on the same thing. Many prayers of agreement have not yielded the expected results simply because the situation was not explained very well. The team must receive enough information to inspire total agreement for the required results.

Sometimes I am tempted to think that this prayer of agreement was designed for families at home. But of course, God always has a bigger picture in all his works. He looked at his own big family on earth, the body of Christ, and saw the gathering of glorified people, a mighty flow of grace, and let us know that nothing can be impossible for us if we set our minds to achieve anything in agreement.

God loves relationships. He enjoys harmony and loves it when the brethren are together in unity and one accord. The bible says, *"there the Lord commanded the blessing, even life for evermore."* (Psalms 133:1-3) There is so much that the family of God can achieve in agreement. Jesus said that just a minimum of two in agreement will receive whatever they will ask the Father in heaven.

He said whenever we are gathered in his name, he is in our midst (Matt 18:20). Many of us can testify to the fact that our lives improved just by attending church regularly. It is not every time we lay hands on the sick to recover; they simply get better for attending the church service. In that church service, if the church could agree concerning anything… nothing can dare stop it from happening.

That's why the spirit of God is so concerned when some give up the habit of gathering together as a family of God. (Hebrews 10:25) Our gatherings are not ordinary, God is in our midst and wherever God is, anything is possible. Yes, it is true when we say God is everywhere, BUT the manifested presence of God is not found everywhere, but in the gathering of his children.

You can't be a born again Christian and say you don't have a church you belong to; God places us in local assemblies as a family to be nurtured to maturity. He gives us ministers of his choice to raise us until we all come to the unity of the faith, unto a perfect man in Christ. (Ephesians 4:11-16)

Some left their churches because they were offended and swore never to step into any church again. That is not excellent for the child of God. Find a solution quickly before the adversary takes advantage of the situation to destroy your righteous soul. There's a solution better than forsaking the assembly of the brethren where your safety is guaranteed.

9

Prayer with fasting

I have always known fasting to be a great and powerful ingredient in prayer, not to make God answer our prayers but rather to help us focus and be able to connect with God's divine power at work in us. *"Now unto him that is able to do exceedingly abundantly above all that we ask or think, according to the power that works in us."* (Ephesians 3:20) Yes, the power of God is in us by the Holy Spirit that dwells in us. We are his living temple (1 Cor 3:16), and this makes our prayer special to God and dynamic in its working (James 5:16). The Holy Spirit's presence in us is the assurance that our prayers will surely produce the desired results.

We however, add fasting to our prayer because fasting helps us to put the body and its pressures to submission so we can easily be in sync with the Holy Spirit and make contact with the power of God. This we do especially when we want to hear specifically from God concerning a matter, or when we desire a deeper fellowship with our father or when the situations of life get tough and rough, requiring a tougher and more rough faith to clear it off.

Fasting doesn't change God, as some have imaged through the years it instead changes us, helping us to focus pay more attention to the spiritual realm, position ourselves correctly.

In fasting, we put away everything, including food, to have fellowship with the Lord alone in prayer. When the body is full, we all know how difficult it can be to concentrate on many things much less spiritual matters. Fasting suspends all the natural senses and allows the spiritual senses to soar higher. The natural cravings are put on hold during fasting, giving way for the spiritual life to dominate.

When fasting, isolation is recommended so that the mind is refocused on what we are praying about. Right there, the spiritual antennas are all alert to send and receive signals. At this time, the natural man is put under subjection, while the spirit man is rising higher in the flow of the spirit's power to make the necessary changes.

It is also important to note that fasting is not only done when we want to turn seemingly hopeless situations around, but fasting is a more necessary and powerful tool for our spiritual growth. As we take time to fellowship with the Holy Spirit in prayer and fasting, our spiritual life is fine-tuned to understand the things of the spirit. We get to know how to function better in that glorious realm of the spirit we are born. The scales of limitation, fear, worry, and anxiety keep falling and fading away in our fellowship with the Spirit, making our Christian life more beautiful and effective as it should be.

You may choose according to your schedule the time and number of days you wish to fast and prayer; and God is ok with that. However, there are moments when the Spirit of God will specifically lead us to fast and pray for a period he may choose and for reasons he may reveal to us or not. Such moments that are inspired of the Holy Spirit should never be negotiated because they normally have a time limit. Beyond the specified time, it might be too late to change anything, or it might require another season which explains the seeming delays in many lives.

The Holy Spirit may prompt you to fast as an individual or speak through your spiritual leader to fast as a group or church. As a member it is very important that you participate in order to partake of the great blessing of corporate prayer and fasting as led by the Holy Spirit.

10

Benefits of prayer

Jesus said that *"men ought to always pray and not to faint"* (Luke 18:1) because he knew the ability of prayer to alter undesirable circumstances of life. Himself as the savior of the world had a habit of prayer (Matt 14:23) and spoke so much about prayer because of the great importance and numerous benefits of prayer.

Prayer is one of those intimate moments with our heavenly father communing together with him in that spiritual fellowship he has called us into (1Cor 1:9). It is this communion with him in prayer that **empowers us and transforms us.** Our lives undergo a transfiguration every time we are in that moment of ministering unto the Lord in holy worship and adoration, making confessions and giving thanks unto his holy name as priests.

In prayer so much is revealed to us enabling us to **know and understand God's will and purpose for our lives**; so that we never walk in the ignorance of life. He says, *"Call unto me and I will answer you and show you great and mighty things which you do not know."* (Jeremiah 33:3) For that matter, the Holy Spirit of God was given to us to guide us into all truth and show us things to come. *"Howbeit when he, the Spirit of truth is come he will guide you into all truth for he shall not speak of himself but whatsoever he shall hear that shall he speak and he will show you things to come."* (John 16:13)

Prayer keeps us motivated and inspired to accomplish our God given dreams and visions. It is not enough that you heard from God concerning those things you want to accomplish for the master, if you don't pray you will soon lose the inspiration and start wondering if you ever heard from the Lord at all. Prayer will keep you on fire, giving you strategies while at the same time opening divine connections to help you accomplish your God given desires. Many have given up on their once much adored dreams and vision because there was no more inspiration. (Romans 12:11)

Prayer creates a spiritual force field around us that keeps enlarging as we continue in prayer consistently. This spiritual force field is an atmosphere of glory around us that releases grace in and around us, attracting good to come to us all the time. When this atmosphere increases continually, everyone that comes in contact with us receives a rub off of that grace around us. We therefore become the very distributors of divine verities everywhere we go as planned by God. **"...for you are a chosen people. You are a kingdom of priests, God's holy nation, his very own possession. <u>This is so you can show others the goodness of God</u>, for he called you out of the darkness into his wonderful light."** (1 Peter 2:9 NLT)

Prayer frustrates, renders powerless, keeps away and destroys completely the enemy's evil plans and strategies against our lives. Jesus said, *"Watch and pray that ye enter not into temptation; the spirit indeed is willing but the flesh is weak"* (Matt 26:41). This lets us know that despite the fact that we know the truth and love to walk in it, we might not do so at the hour of temptation because the flesh is weak. Therefore, Jesus instructs us to watch and pray so that we will not fall into the devil's trap and be sorry after. Prayer will cut off the devil's plans and when we find ourselves in the middle of it, we will not be weak but strong giving glory to God.

There are countless blessings and benefits of prayer that can never be exhausted. The master was not joking when he said men ought always to pray and not faint because *"with God all things are possible"* (Matt 19:26)

Prayer of Salvation

In case you have been reading this book and you are not yet born again, or you had walked away from the faith, now is the time to put things right with God. We believe this is your appointed time to receive this precious gift of eternal life and start a personal relationship with God almighty by wholeheartedly repeating the confession below:

Dear Father, thank you for loving me so much that you sent your only begotten son; that if I believe in him, I should never perish but have everlasting life.

Father as your word says that if we shall confess with our mouth the Lord Jesus and shall believe in our hearts that you have raised him from the dead, we shall be saved According to Romans 10:9; I right now confess with my mouth that Jesus is my lord and savior because I believe in my heart that he died for me and you raised him from the dead for my salvation. I receive the forgiveness of all my sins today.

Thank you, dear father, for saving my life and for the precious gift of eternal life I have received now through Jesus Christ. I declare that I am born again. I am your child with your nature and life in me.

I belong to your kingdom now. I am a new creature, the old is gone, the new has come and all the new in me now is from you my God, in Jesus mighty name. Amen.

Congratulations! You are now a child of God. You can reach us for more information through the contact address in this book. God richly bless you!

www.ingramcontent.com/pod-product-compliance
Lightning Source LLC
LaVergne TN
LVHW081337060426
835513LV00014B/1324